GEOGRAPHY Y4 / P5

Teacher's Notes
Improving the Environment

Gill Howell

Series editor | Sue Palmer

Contents

OXFORD
UNIVERSITY PRESS

OXFORD
UNIVERSITY PRESS

Great Clarendon Street, Oxford OX2 6DP

Oxford University Press is a department of the University of Oxford.
It furthers the University's objective of excellence in research, scholarship,
and education by publishing worldwide in

Oxford New York

Auckland Cape Town Dar es Salaam Hong Kong Karachi
Kuala Lumpur Madrid Melbourne Mexico City Nairobi
New Delhi Shanghai Taipei Tornoto

With offices in

Argentina Austria Brazil Chile Czech Republic France Greece
Guatemala Hungary Italy Japan Poland Portugal Singapore
South Korea Switzerland Thailand Turkey Ukraine Vietnam

Oxford is a registered trade mark of Oxford University Press
in the UK and in certain other countries

British Library Cataloguing in Publication Data

Data available

ISBN-13: 978-0-19-834871-9
ISBN-10: 0-19-834871-1

7 9 10 8

Typeset by Fakenham Photosetting, Fakenham, Norfolk

Printed in the UK

What is Oxford Connections?

Oxford Connections is a set of 12 cross-curricular books and related teaching materials for 7 to 11 year olds. The books will help you teach literacy through a science, geography or history-based topic. Each book provides the material to cover one unit from the QCA Schemes of Work for the National Curriculum in England and Wales, and the non-fiction literacy objectives for one whole year of the National Literacy Strategy. (You can find a grid of where the QCA and NLS objectives are covered on p 48 of these notes and on the inside back cover of the pupils' books.) The books can be used to focus primarily on literacy or on science/geography/history.

Literacy

Pupils need different literacies. As well as traditional texts with different purposes and audiences, they also need to be able to understand and write material presented in different forms such as diagrams, bullet points, notes and Internet displays, particularly when working with non-fiction.

Oxford Connections supports the development of these different literacies. It focuses particularly on reading and writing non-fiction, and will help pupils use effectively the different non-fiction text types (report, explanation, instructions, recount, discussion, persuasion).

Using these books will help pupils to focus on the two main elements which make a text type what it is:

◆ The language features used (for example, present tense for instructions, and past tense for recounts, use of commands in instructions).
◆ The structure of the text (for example, chronological order, in the case of instructions or recounts).

The structure of a text can be represented as a diagram or framework, showing visually how the parts of the text fit together, which are the main points and how they are developed. (A very common example of this type of presentation is a timeline, which shows events which have happened in the past, as a continuum, the order of which cannot change.) In these notes, we refer to material presented in this diagrammatic way as *visual* (*visual reports*, *visual explanations*, etc.).

Pupils will learn to read and to present information visually (by using frameworks), thus developing good note-taking skills, and consolidating their understanding of how texts are structured. The visual texts, in particular, are accessible to those pupils who need more support. Using frameworks to plan their own writing will also help to improve all pupils' planning and drafting/editing skills.

In these notes, we have used icons to represent the different sorts of frameworks you can use, called *skeletons*. These are referred to in the *National Literacy Strategy Support Materials for Text Level Objectives* (DfES 0532/2001). They can be used as an aide-memoire to help pupils remember the structure of each text type. They appear on pp 6–47 to show you what text types are on the pupils' book pages.

Recount		Explanation	
Instructions		Persuasion	
Non-chronological report		Discussion	

Using *Improving the Environment* to teach literacy

There are step-by-step instructions to teach pupils how to read and write the different text types, on pp 18–47 (a six-page section for each text type). They follow this model:

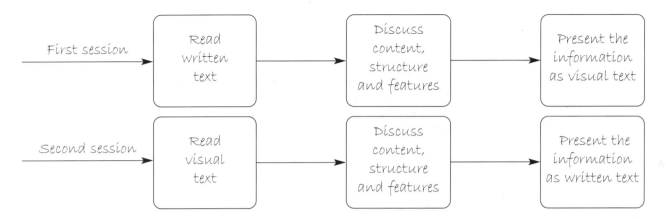

Each six-page section contains:

Two pages of step-by-step instructions taking you through the process described in the diagram above. They will help you analyse a written text, and then produce a visual version of that text with a group of pupils. You will then analyse a visual text, producing a written version.

A page describing the relevant text type.*

An example of the text type (an excerpt from *Improving the Environment*) for you to read and analyse with pupils.*

The same example with language features highlighted for your reference.*

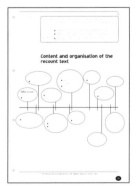

A visual version of the written text for your reference.*

these notes can be photocopied as handouts, a poster or an OHT

There are page-by-page notes on how to use the material to cover other aspects of literacy on pp 6–17. These page-by-page notes also show how to use the material in the pupils' book for the particular subject covered, e.g. geography.

Speaking and listening, and drama

The discussion which is inherent in this method of learning should improve pupils' speaking and listening skills. As well as helping pupils to organize and structure their ideas before writing, visual texts should prompt pupils to use the relevant language features orally, as well as in writing. Additional speaking and listening, and drama activities such as those below, can be used to further reinforce the pupils' learning.

Retelling – events can be retold by an individual or by groups taking a section from a visual recount.

Role-play – using the visuals created by the whole class to ask/answer questions in role, e.g. as the person in the recount or as someone taking one side of the argument.

Mini plays – retelling an event or following an explanation visual to show how something works. Pupils could be the different parts of whatever is being explained.

Puppet plays – retelling an event or following an explanation visual.

Freeze-frame – pupils in groups could show sections from a recount visual or report visual. They could show different aspects of a discussion.

TV/radio reports – demonstrating knowledge using a visual report as a TV/radio report. In a TV report images could be used either pictorially or by the use of freeze framing.

TV demonstrations – following an instruction visual or explanation visual to demonstrate making something or explaining how something works.

TV/radio interviews – retelling events in recounts or using report visuals while interviewing another pupil/pupils in role.

TV/radio adverts – using a persuasive visual to make adverts.

Illustrated talks – using the visual as a prompt.

Hot seat – answering questions in role – either as a persuasion, report or recount.

Debates – using discussion visuals to have debates between individuals or groups.

Using *Improving the Environment* to teach geography

Improving the Environment contains all the material you need to cover this topic, and to achieve the objectives of the *QCA Scheme of Work for the National Curriculum Geography Unit 8* (recommended for Year 4 pupils). There are page-by-page notes on how to use the material for geography on pp 6–17. You can find a grid showing how the QCA objectives are covered on p 48 of these notes, and on the inside back cover of *Improving the Environment* pupils' book.

Which year group should I use *Improving the Environment* with?

Improving the Environment has been written for Year 4 pupils (8–9 year olds). However, if your school places the topic in another year group, the geography material contained in *Improving the Environment* will still be suitable for use with other age groups. Although all of the non-fiction literacy objectives for Year 4 are covered, many of the objectives for other year groups are also supported. Most of the six non-fiction text types are covered in it, and language features for Years 3, 5 and 6 are highlighted in the relevant sections.

NB Throughout this introduction the term Year 4 has been used to mean 8–9 year olds. The references in the grid on p 48 are to the *National Literacy Strategy* and to the *QCA Scheme of Work for the National Curriculum*. However, *Improving the*

SCOTLAND AND NORTHERN IRELAND

Environment is suitable for use with P5 in Scotland and in Northern Ireland, since it supports many elements of the *National Guidelines, 5–14* and *The Northern Ireland Curriculum*. The geography content of *Improving the Environment* does not conflict in any way with either *National Guidelines, 5–14* or *The Northern Ireland Curriculum*.

Pages 2–3

Geography

Use these pages as advance organizers to provide pupils with an overview of the work to be carried out:

concept map shows the main areas to be covered and links between them.

contents page shows how information has been organized in the book.

◆ Use the quotation as an aide for using the contents page – ask pupils to find what is being mentioned.
◆ Return to the pages occasionally during teaching to help the pupils see how their learning and understanding is developing.
◆ Use these pages as a revision aid when you want to review what has been learned. This will help to show pupils the progress they are making in their learning.
◆ Use the concept map at the end of the topic to review all areas of the topic covered.

Literacy

◆ Establish the links between the concept map and the contents page. Look at similarities and differences between them (e.g. they contain the same information but organized differently; the concept map provides an overview of the ideas in the book, the contents page provides an ordered guide to what the book contains).
◆ Let pupils practise finding information using the contents page and index until they are confident enough to find requested information quickly.

Pages 4–5

Geography

Key concept
◆ To ask and respond to geographical questions.

Key vocabulary
◆ *environment, atmosphere, Earth, air, water*

Suggested activities
◆ Pupils in pairs investigate small environments within the whole environment of the school or classroom, and list any life-forms they find.
◆ Pupils make a chart or table to compare and contrast these environments. (Link to Maths/ICT)
◆ Pupils draw a chart to classify the environments by size, temperature, light/dark, dry/wet. (Link to Science QCA Unit 4B)

Literacy

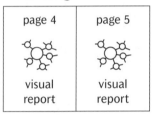

page 4	page 5
visual report	visual report

◆ Read opening paragraph and discuss its purpose.
◆ In pairs, discuss which parts of the skeleton could be used as headings in a written report.
◆ Identify the different environments to include under the headings and what information to include, and what to ignore.
◆ Collaborate with the class to write the outline of a report that will be used as a template.
◆ Brainstorm a new opening sentence.
◆ Discuss what sort of vocabulary will be used, e.g. tense, technical vocabulary, generalized nouns.
◆ Pupils re-write the information into a written report text using the template outline as a model.
◆ Ask pupils to check the vocabulary they have used by referring to the text to check for accuracy of spelling.

Geography

Key concepts
◆ How people affect the environment.
◆ How and why people seek to manage and sustain their environment.

Key vocabulary
◆ *landfills, quarries, leachate, carbon dioxide, methane, sewage, site, incinerator*

Suggested activities
◆ Before reading the text, ask the pupils to describe what happens to their rubbish when the dustbins are collected.
◆ Read the text and list the disadvantages of landfill sites.
◆ Discuss whether pupils have seen a landfill site. If they have ask them to describe what it was like and where the site was. (Usually unpopulated areas.)

Literacy

page 14	page 15
○→☼→○	○→☼→○
written explanation	written explanation

These pages are used as a featured example to teach the reading and writing of **explanation** text (see pp 30–35 of these teacher's notes).

Also use to:

◆ Plan and write a letter to a district council from a rural community who do not want plans for a landfill site near their village to go ahead.

Geography

Key concepts
◆ How and why people seek to manage and sustain their environment.
◆ To collect and record evidence to answer questions.

Key vocabulary
◆ *resurface, porous asphalt, vehicle, divert, highway maintenance, Borough Council*

Suggested activities
◆ Discuss the two issues in the email and letter.
◆ Ask the pupils to discuss in pairs which issue they feel is the most important.
◆ Pupils report back with reasons for their opinions.
◆ Draw a chart to illustrate the class's opinion.
◆ Discuss the different methods the two children chose to express their complaint.
◆ Ask the pupils to write an email about a local problem to a friend. (Link to ICT QCA Unit 4A)

Literacy

page 16	page 17
*⚡ *⚡ *⚡	*⚡ *⚡ *⚡
written persuasion	written persuasion

These pages are used as a featured example to teach the reading and writing of **persuasion** text (see pp 36–41 of these teacher's notes).

Use also to teach that the format and tone of letters and emails depends upon the audience and purpose.

◆ Pupils re-write the email to Sophie as a letter to Sophie's father.
◆ Pupils re-write the letter to Morton Borough Council as an email.

Geography

Key concepts
- How and why people seek to manage and sustain their environment.
- To collect and record evidence to answer questions.

Key vocabulary
- *consumer, recycling, reprocessing*

Suggested activities
- Pupils convert the list of the contents of an average bin into a graph or pie chart. (Link to Maths/ ICT QCA Unit 4D)
- Collect the contents of the class waste bin and compare the percentages of its contents with the graphs.
- Using other sources, including ICT, pupils find out how aluminium cans are recycled, and display the information as a cyclical flowchart.

Literacy

pages 18	page 19
○→☼→☼	○→☼→☼
visual explanation	visual explanation

These pages are used as a featured example to teach the reading and writing of **explanation** text (see pp 30–35 of these teacher's notes).

Also use to:

- Ask pupils to design and write persuasive posters encouraging people to recycle paper.

Geography

Key concepts
- How and why people seek to manage and sustain their environment.
- To collect and record evidence to answer questions.

Key vocabulary
- *compost, recycling, raw materials, glasphalt, fibre, insulation*

Suggested activities
- Read the instructions and the news report, and discuss what is being recycled, and how it is being used.
- Ask pupils to look out for any uses of recycled resources in the local area.
- Pupils use the Internet to search for other unusual and imaginative ways resources are recycled into new raw materials. (Link to ICT)
- Pupils in pairs design a new way to use one of the following: cans, bottles and jars, jumpers or cardigans. (Link to Design and Technology)

Literacy

page 20	Page 21
○→○→○→	☼
written instruction	written report

Page 20
- List the features of the instruction text (imperative verbs, chronological, short sentences).
- Discuss the layout of the instruction text, and list the devices that are used, e.g. numbered lists, bullet points.
- Re-write the diagram of the worm bin as a flow chart.

Page 21
- List the features of this news report (see p 26 of these notes).
- Note that the report is presented in a journalistic style.
- Use the ideas for recycling from pupils' own ideas to draft their own newspaper report.
- Prepare finished reports using a computer program. (Link to ICT)

Geography

Key concepts
♦ To collect and record evidence to answer questions.
♦ How and why people seek to manage and sustain their environment.

Key vocabulary
♦ *pollution, raw materials, Clean Air Act, hybrid engines, fuel cells, smog*

Suggested activities
♦ Find out two facts about James Watt and George Stephenson. (Link to History)
♦ Hold a class survey. Ask parents/carers and friends what they do to avoid polluting the atmosphere.
♦ Write up the class findings and work out the proportions of people who take action, e.g. share cars, use public transport, burn smokeless fuel, etc. (Link to Maths)

Literacy

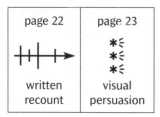

page 22	page 23
written recount	visual persuasion

♦ Discuss the main point of each paragraph in the written recount.
♦ Revise the main features of recount text (see p 20 of these notes) and the basic skeleton used to make notes.
♦ Ask pupils to prepare notes on the text using a timeline skeleton.
♦ Use the visual persuasion as a stimulus to design a persuasive poster on traffic pollution. (Link to Art and Design/IT)
♦ Revise the language features and style of persuasion text (see p 38 of these teacher's notes).
♦ Discuss persuasion text features for the pupils' own posters, e.g. emotive language, use of different font effects, etc.

Geography

Key concepts
♦ To ask and respond to geographical questions.
♦ To collect and record evidence to answer questions.
♦ How people affect the environment.
♦ How and why people seek to manage and sustain their environment.

Key vocabulary
♦ *global warming, atmosphere, gravity, radiation, carbon dioxide, methane, greenhouse gas, renewable energy, climate change*

Suggested activities
♦ In pairs, pupils write six questions for a quiz about global warming. Pairs swap quizzes and answer the questions.
♦ Use a thermometer to measure the temperature in a sunny part of the playground, and a shaded part. Describe what causes any differences in temperature. (Link to Science QCA Unit 4C)
♦ Write a definition of the Greenhouse Effect in less than 30 words.

Literacy

page 24	page 25
written discussion	written discussion
written explanation	written explanation

♦ Write notes of key points using a discussion skeleton.
♦ Identify and list which points are fact and which are opinion.
♦ Using the information in Meena's emails, write an explanation text for a new audience.
♦ In pairs, note the key points using an explanation skeleton.
♦ Discuss the relative merits of written text and diagrams for conveying information.

Geography

Key concepts
◆ To collect and record evidence to answer questions.
◆ To investigate places.

Key vocabulary
◆ *methane, pollen, bacteria, air pollution, atmosphere*

Suggested activities
◆ Discuss, in pairs, which natural air pollution problem they think has the most impact on people's lives in general, and themselves personally.
◆ List the effects of a) pollen b) volcanoes c) dust storms.
◆ Ask pupils to imagine what it would be like to be affected by one of the features of the visual report, and then write a sentence describing how they would feel.

Literacy

page 26	page 27
visual report	visual report
written report	journalistic recount

◆ Ask pupils to choose two of the topics that appear in note form and to write them up as a written report following the example 'marsh gas'.
◆ Write notes on the recount text, 'Krakatoa', picking out key points and writing the notes using a recount skeleton (see p 23 of these notes).

Geography

Key concepts
◆ To ask and respond to geographical questions.
◆ To collect and record evidence to answer questions.
◆ How people affect the environment.
◆ How and why people seek to manage and sustain their environment.

Key vocabulary
sewage treatment, pollution, oil

Suggested activities
◆ List forms of pollution in a) rivers, b) beaches.
◆ Identify and list rivers near the school.
◆ Visit a local river or beach and make notes on any visible pollution.
◆ Research coastline pollution caused by oil tankers. Use ICT and newspapers to find out about other major oil spillages, their location and effect. (Link to History)
◆ Pupils prepare and act out a play describing life living beside the Thames in Victorian times. (Link to Drama)

Literacy

page 28	page 29
visual recount	visual recount

◆ List the features of recount text, i.e. chronological structure, scene setting and closing statement. Plus use of past tense, time markers and action words.
◆ In pairs, pupils make notes and write a journalistic recount for a newspaper based on the information in 'Oil spill alert'.
◆ Use ICT to present the article in a newspaper style.
◆ Discuss the points raised in 'Cleaning up the River Thames'. In pairs, pupils make notes and write a recount describing life living beside the Thames in London, from the nineteenth century up to the twentieth century, describing the changes. Link in with the drama suggestion above.

Geography

Key concepts
- To ask and respond to geographical questions.
- How people affect the environment.
- To collect and record evidence to answer questions.
- To use ICT to present findings.

Key vocabulary
- *planning permission, housing developments, pollution, fertilizers, pesticides*

Suggested activities
- Discuss the effect that the increasing population has on transport, housing and food.
- Ask pupils, in pairs, to discuss why they think big fields without hedges can be bad for wildlife. (Link to Science QCA Unit 4B)
- List points for and against big out-of-town shopping centres.

Literacy

page 30	page 31
written report	visual explanation

- List the causal connectives used in the report.
- In pairs, compose a single sentence to summarize the main point of the report text having organized the information in a skeleton.
- Use the information in the pie chart to write a report text on land use in 1995.
- Discuss using the visual explanation to write a written explanation (see pp 30–35 of these notes).
- Brainstorm writing opening statements.
- Ask pupils to identify how to group information into paragraphs.
- Demonstrate writing an opening paragraph, and discuss connectives to use.
- Pupils finish the explanation independently.

Geography

Key concepts
- How people affect the environment.
- How and why people seek to manage and sustain their environment.

Key vocabulary
- *poachers, conservationists, game reserves, protected areas*

Suggested activities
- Read and discuss the information in the text with the pupils.
- Brainstorm a list of other endangered species.
- Discuss what pupils already know about endangered animals from their own experience. (Link to Science)
- In pairs, write bullet points for one new animal from their own list using the three headings: Facts, Dangers, Actions.

Literacy

page 32	page 33
written report	visual report
visual report	

These pages are used as a featured example to teach the reading and writing of **report** text (see pp 24–29 of these teacher's notes).

Also use to:

- Discuss the impact of bullet-pointed information and compare this with narrative text.

Geography

Key concepts
◆ How and why people seek to manage and sustain their environment.
◆ To investigate places.

Key vocabulary
◆ *United Nations, Earth Summit, environment, World Wide Fund, national parks, reserves*

Suggested activities
◆ Read the two newspaper reports and discuss how international agencies are involved in conservation and improving the environment.
◆ Compose a sentence to say what the difference is between the proposed actions described.
◆ Use the Greenpeace persuasion text to write a newspaper article about Greenpeace. (Link to ICT QCA Unit 4C)
◆ Look through newspapers and magazines for international organizations tackling world environment issues. Make a display using a world map.

Literacy

Page 34	page 35
written report	written persuasion

◆ Note that the reports are presented in journalistic style.
◆ Brainstorm actions that could be taken to improve the school environment.
◆ In pairs, draft the layout of a newspaper article outlining the school improvements.
◆ Use a computer program to present the article in the style of a newspaper.
◆ Pupils present key points of the persuasion texts as persuasion skeletons.
◆ In pairs, pupils use the skeleton notes to design and write a poster advertising one of the organizations.

Geography

Key concept
◆ How and why people seek to manage and sustain their environment.

Key vocabulary
◆ *biodiversity, wildlife, habitat, action plan, flagship species*

Suggested activities
◆ Read and discuss the Chelmsford action plan.
◆ Pairs of pupils list wildlife habitats in the local area. (Link to Science QCA Unit 4B)
◆ Pairs of pupils research local conservation groups using ICT, the library and local knowledge.
◆ Pairs of pupils make notes for drawing up an action plan for the local area.

Literacy

Page 36	page 37
written report	visual report
visual report	

◆ In pairs, pupils write notes in preparation for writing a TV news report on the Chelmsford action plan using the information in the written report and the skeleton.
◆ Discuss the key points to be included.
◆ As a class, brainstorm headlines for the news report.
◆ In groups, pupils write and present their news report. (Link to Drama)

Geography

Key concepts
◆ How and why people seek to manage and sustain their environment.
◆ To collect and record evidence to answer questions.

Key vocabulary
◆ *wildlife, habitat, compost*

Suggested activities
◆ List the different environments within a wildlife garden.
◆ List the different species of wildlife that might be found in a wildlife garden. (Link to Science QCA Unit 4B)
◆ Discuss how individual people can improve their local environment, and the effect this might have on the wider environment.

Literacy

page 38	page 39
○►○►○►	○►○►○►
visual instruction	visual instruction

◆ Discuss the main language features of instruction text: imperative verbs; numbered points; short, clear sentences; chronological, etc.
◆ Discuss what is happening in each illustration of the visual instruction.
◆ Ask pupils, in pairs, to write the visual instruction as written text.
◆ Model writing the first step, e.g. 1. Use a pencil and paper to draw a plan of the garden.
◆ Ask half the class to write up instructions for building a wildlife garden, and the other half to write instructions for building a wildlife pond.

Geography

Key concepts
◆ To collect and record evidence to answer questions.
◆ How and why people seek to manage their environment.
◆ To investigate places.
◆ To ask and respond to geographical questions.
◆ How people affect the environment.

Key vocabulary
◆ *planet, wildlife, conservation*

Suggested activities
◆ Discuss the purpose of each of the advertisements.
◆ Pupils list the different environments that each advertisement is promoting.
◆ In pairs, each pupil can choose an advertisement and through role-play, promote its cause.
◆ As a class, discuss which cause the pupils feel most strongly about.

Literacy

page 40	page 41
*⌇ *⌇ *⌇	*⌇ *⌇ *⌇
visual persuasion	visual persuasion

These pages are used as a featured example to teach the reading and writing of **persuasion** text (see pp 36–41 of these teacher's notes).

Geography

Key concepts
- How and why people seek to manage and sustain their environment.
- To collect and record evidence to answer questions.
- To investigate places.
- To ask and respond to geographical questions.
- How people affect the environment.

Suggested activities
- In pairs, list the different environments that the pupils use during one week.
- In groups, discuss one of these environments, and how it could be improved.
- List the problems in one column, with ideas for improvement in another column.

Literacy

page 42	page 43
visual report	written discussion

Page 42
- Use the visual report as a stimulus to write a written report. Each circle on the skeleton becomes one paragraph (see pp 24–29 of these notes).

Page 43
These pages are used as a featured example to teach the reading and writing of **discussion** text (see pp 42–47 of these teacher's notes).

Geography

Key concepts
- How people affect the environment.
- How and why people seek to manage and sustain their environment.
- To investigate places.

Key vocabulary
- *resources, atmosphere, climate*

Suggested activities
- Discuss the features of Earth that are visible from space.
- Talk about the environmental concerns each of the children featured might have.
- Read and discuss the different ways the environment is being damaged.
- Ask pupils to write one example for each of the ways the environment is being damaged.
- In pairs, draw up a list of actions individual pupils can take to help sustain the environment.

Literacy

page 44	page 45
visual report	written persuasion

- Pupils write a letter or email on behalf of one of the children featured outlining their environmental concerns. The correspondence could be directed to an imaginary government official.
- List the features of persuasion text (see p 38 of these notes).
- Read the second paragraph. In pairs, pupils draw up a list of questions for finding out more about the environment. (Link to ICT QCA Unit 4D)
- In pairs, pupils design and write a flyer to encourage other pupils to take an active part in improving the environment.
- Investigate the way punctuation has been used in complex sentences.

Page 46

Geography

Key concept

◆ To ask and respond to geographical questions.

Suggested activity

◆ Use these pages to search for the meanings of key vocabulary to further the pupils' understanding of different aspects of the environment. Identify words from reading that are unknown and use the glossary to further understanding and to clarify information learnt.

Literacy

Use these pages to demonstrate how to locate information confidently and efficiently using a glossary.

Remind pupils of the purpose of a glossary: to explain the meaning of words to the reader and of any words or terms that are specific to the subject of the text.

Using some of the key words identified in both the text and these notes, scan the glossary to find some of the meanings. Point out that the words are in alphabetical order rather than subject order.

Page 47-48

Geography

Key concept

◆ To collect and record evidence to answer questions.

Literacy

Use these pages to teach the pupils the purpose and function of a **bibliography** and an index.

Point out to pupils that a bibliography:

◆ collates all the references to other sources made in the text;
◆ provides a reference point for further reading;
◆ is organized alphabetically using the surname of the author;
◆ sometimes provides the ISBN number as well as the title of the reference;
◆ contains some of the following sources: books, websites, articles, periodicals and journals.

Use the bibliography to find further details about one area of improving the environment. Ensure the pupils use a wide range of sources referenced.

Discuss how different source material, e.g. websites, books, are organized. Compare details provided in *Improving the Environment* with material found in a different source.

Point out that an index is organized alphabetically, giving page numbers. Encourage pupils to practise skimming and scanning text to locate the index word on the page referred to.

Teaching pupils how to read and write journalistic recounts

page 12

journalistic
recount

Reading a recount text in journalistic style

Read the newspaper extract on p 12 of *Improving the Environment* pupils' book. You will need:

- the written recount on p 12 (the text-only version on p 21 of these notes can be enlarged/photocopied/made into an OHT for annotation);
- p 20 of these notes enlarged/photocopied/made into an OHT for annotation.

SHARED READING ACTIVITY

Audience and purpose
Note how the intended audience and purpose affects language and layout.

Audience – general readers who are interested in knowing about the topic or event.

Purpose – to provide information about a topic or event.

SHARED WRITING ACTIVITY

Content and organization
Revise the content and help pupils understand how journalistic recount is organized by demonstrating its content in a recount skeleton (see p 23 of these notes).

SHARED READING ACTIVITY

Language features and style
Return to the text and help pupils understand how the language has been used to achieve the effects the author intended (see annotated example on p 22 of these notes).

PAIRED READING ACTIVITY

Pupils discuss writing a closing paragraph for the newspaper article.

INDEPENDENT ACTIVITY

Pairs of pupils role play being the reporter and the witness, acting out the scene described in the newspaper article.

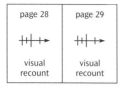

page 28	page 29
visual recount	visual recount

Writing a recount text

Use pp 28–29 of *Improving the Environment* pupils' book as a basis for pupils' own recount texts. You will need:

◆ the visual recounts on pp 28–29;
◆ p 20 of these notes enlarged/photocopied/made into an OHT for annotation.

Content and organization

> SHARED
> READING AND
> WRITING
> ACTIVITY

Revise the content and organization of the recount text from the previous session (see p 18 of these notes).

Read the timeline notes with pupils, and discuss how information is presented in note form. Ask pupils to work in pairs to translate one note into a longer sentence adding information as appropriate.

Language features and style

Revise the main features of recount text (see p 20 of these notes) and discuss the writing task.

Audience and purpose

> SHARED
> READING
> ACTIVITY

Discuss the audience for pupils' recounts (readers who would like to know more about either cleaning up the Thames or the *Sea Empress* oil spill disaster) and the purpose (to retell events).

> SHARED
> WRITING
> ACTIVITY

Using information on the timelines, demonstrate how to expand key ideas into coherent sentences to write a recount of either cleaning up the Thames or the *Sea Empress* oil spill diasaster. Demonstrate how to organize each paragraph, e.g.

On the 15 February 1996, the oil tanker Sea Empress *ran aground at the entrance to Milford Haven harbour. She was loaded with 131,000 tonnes of crude oil. Immediately the oil began to spill into the sea ...*

> INDEPENDENT
> WRITING
> ACTIVITY

Ask pupils to use whiteboards to compose the next two sentences ensuring that they continue writing in the past tense.

Pupils complete the recount independently.

About journalistic recount text

Audience and purpose

Audience – someone who may not know much about the events.

Purpose – to retell events that actually happened.

Sometimes you may know more about the age or interests of your reader

Content and organization

◆ **headline** uses brief language, often summarizes the content

◆ **introductory paragraph** sets the scene, so the reader has all the basic facts needed to understand the recount

Answer the questions who? what? when? where?

◆ **introduction** often also expands the headline to tell the main event of the recount

Use your introductory sentence to help you write your conclusion. If the introduction is a question then answer it in your conclusions

◆ events written in **chronological order** – time order

◆ **closing statement** – sentence(s) or paragraph to bring the recount to an end

First this happened … then this happened … next …

Language features

◆ written in the **past tense** because these are specific events that only happened once

First …, next …, finally …, In 1950 …, Some weeks later …

◆ focus on **specific people, places, dates,** etc.

◆ usually written in the **third person**

◆ **words and devices** to show **time order**

This usually means proper nouns, so remember the capital letters!

◆ **passive verb forms,** often with a hidden agent

◆ a mixture of direct and indirect speech for **quotations**

Was knocked down … The reporter was told …

The basic skeleton for making notes is a timeline

An example of a newspaper recount

Boy on bike hurt

By Ivor Penn

Gary Smellifeet (9) was knocked off his bike in New Road last Tuesday at 5.30 pm, in yet another accident on the Lionsway Estate. Gary's mother explained he was a very careful cyclist. She added, 'The problem is the traffic – there's too much of it and it's going too fast.'

Mrs Kerry White (34), who witnessed the accident, said, 'The boy just skidded right in front of the car. The driver didn't have a chance. The problem is the kids – they shouldn't be allowed to cycle round here. Everyone uses New Road as a shortcut to get round the traffic jams at the lights on the main road.'

Language features and style of the newspaper recount

Boy on bike hurt

By Ivor Penn

Gary Smellifeet (9) was knocked off his bike in New Road last Tuesday at 5.30 pm, in yet another accident on the Lionsway Estate. Gary's mother explained he was a very careful cyclist. She added, 'The problem is the traffic – there's too much of it and it's going too fast.'

Mrs Kerry White (34), who witnessed the accident, said, 'The boy just skidded off the pavement, right in front of the car. The driver didn't have a chance. The problem is the kids – they shouldn't be allowed to cycle round here. Everyone uses New Road as a shortcut to get round the traffic jams at the lights on the main road.'

Past tense verbs

Specific people 'Who'

Specific place 'Where'

Detail to add interest

- Bold headline to get readers' attention
- Summarizes content

Specific time 'When'

Mixture of reported and direct quotations to add interest

Content and organization of the recount text

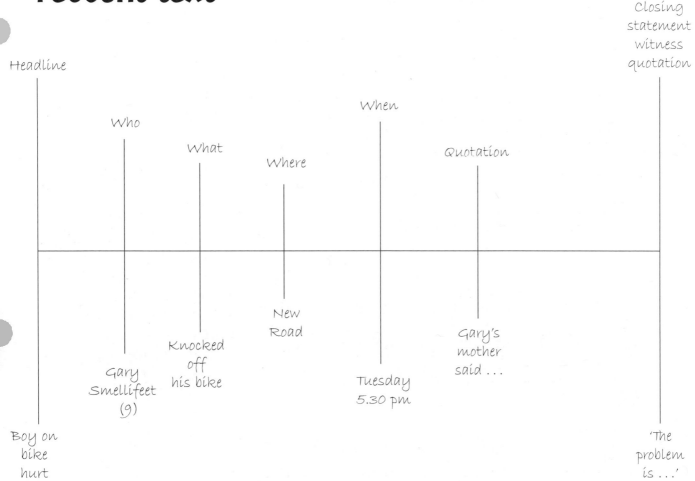

Teaching pupils how to read and write report text

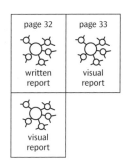

page 32	page 33
written report	visual report
visual report	

Reading a report text

Read pp 32–33 of *Improving the Environment* pupils' book with the pupils. You will need:

- the report text on pp 32–33 (the text-only version on p 27 of these notes can be enlarged/photocopied/made into an OHT for annotation);
- p 26 of these notes enlarged/photocopied/made into an OHT for annotation.

SHARED READING ACTIVITY

Audience and purpose

Talk about how the intended audience and purpose affects language and layout.

Audience – pupils who may know little about endangered animals.

Purpose – to give brief information about four endangered species.

Content and organization

SHARED WRITING ACTIVITY

Show the pupils how the content of this report text is organized by showing its content in a report skeleton (see p 29 of these notes). The organization is non-chronological, with information grouped into paragraphs by content. Each circle becomes one paragraph, linked by arms with details noted around it.

PAIRED WRITING ACTIVITY

Ask pupils, in pairs, to quickly organize the bullet-pointed information on African elephants into a report skeleton to ensure they understand the organization of report text, e.g.

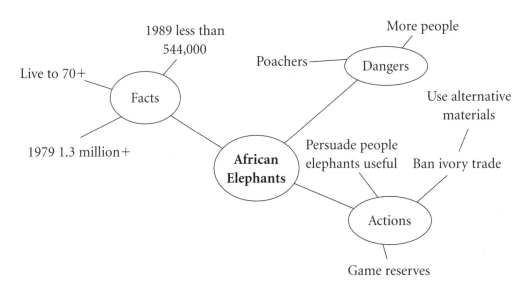

SHARED READING ACTIVITY

Language features and style

Return to the text and talk about how language has been used to achieve the effect the author intended. (See annotated version on p 28 of these notes.)

Discuss how elements of explanation text are sometimes incorporated into reports, to ensure readers understand the topic.

Note useful features for use in pupils' own writing, e.g. subject shifts denoted by new paragraphs, variation in connective devices – *The main reason, Another problem, A further danger.*

INDEPENDENT ACTIVITY

In pairs, talk about other animals they think might be endangered, and each think of one action that could be taken to help conserve the species.

page 32
written report

visual report

Writing a report text

Use the section on tigers on p 32 of *Improving the Environment* pupil's book as a basis for pupils' own report texts. You will need:

- the visual report on p 32;
- p 26 of these notes enlarged/photocopied/made into an OHT for annotation.

Content and organization

Revise the content and organization of the report text from the previous session (see p 24 of these notes).

PAIRED READING AND WRITING ACTIVITY

Pairs of pupils read and discuss the bullet-pointed information in the section on tigers (p 32), and make notes as shown in the report skeleton. Notes should be organized by paragraph, with any other information they wish to add grouped around each circle.

Discuss the notes.

Language features and style

Remind pupils of the language features of report text (see p 26 of these notes).

Audience and purpose

SHARED READING ACTIVITY

Discuss the audience for pupils' reports (readers who know nothing about endangered animals) and the purpose (to give readers basic information about the danger to tigers and how to reduce it).

SHARED WRITING ACTIVITY

Demonstrate writing a title for the report. Ask for suggestions from the pupils, e.g. *Tigers in Danger, Saving the Tiger*.

Discuss writing an introductory sentence, e.g. *Tigers are the largest wild cats in the world.*

Discuss how much information should be included in the opening paragraph. Scribe the opening paragraph using suggestions from the pupils.

Draw up a list of suitable connectives with the pupils.

INDEPENDENT WRITING ACTIVITY

Pupils write the remaining paragraphs independently.

About report text

Audience and purpose

Audience – someone who wants to know about the topic.

Purpose – to describe what something is like.

> Sometimes you may know more about the age or interests of your reader

Content and organization

- **non-chronological** information
- **introductory sentence or paragraph** says what the report is going to be about
- the information is sorted into groups or **categories**
- reports may include short pieces of explanation

> This means it ISN'T written in time order, like a story or recount

> What something looks like, where it is found . . .

Language features

- written in the **present tense**
- usually **general nouns and pronouns** (not particular people or things)
- **factual descriptive words**, not like the descriptions in a story
- words and devices that show **comparison and contrast**
- **third person** writing to make the report **impersonal and formal**
- **technical words and phrases** – which you may need to explain to the reader
- use of **examples** to help the reader understand the technical words

> You would write about dogs in general, not a particular dog

> You would say powerful beams, not beautiful bright beams

> Expressions like have in common, the same as . . ., on the other hand, however. . .

> Unusual words that go with the topic such as canine, translucent and wing span

> Wingspan is the distance between the tips of a bird's outstretched wings

The basic skeleton for making notes is a spidergram

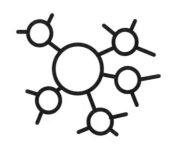

An example of a report text

Giant pandas

Giant pandas live in bamboo clumps on steep mountain slopes in China. They eat mainly bamboo shoots. Sadly, there are probably now fewer than 1000 left in the wild.

The main reason that giant pandas are endangered is that people are chopping down the bamboo forests, and so the panda's food supplies are running out. Another problem is that giant pandas live in family groups in small patches of forest, and so it is difficult for them to meet other pandas, to breed and have cubs. A further danger comes from poachers, who kill and capture the giant pandas.

In order to save the giant pandas, conservationists need to study them in order to find out their exact numbers, and how they live. This will help us know what they need to survive. One thing that can be done is to plant special strips of bamboo forest (called panda-corridors). These link one patch of forest with another so that pandas can meet more easily. Also, more panda reserves can be set up. In the reserves, trained staff protect and look after the pandas.

Language features and style of the report text

Giant pandas

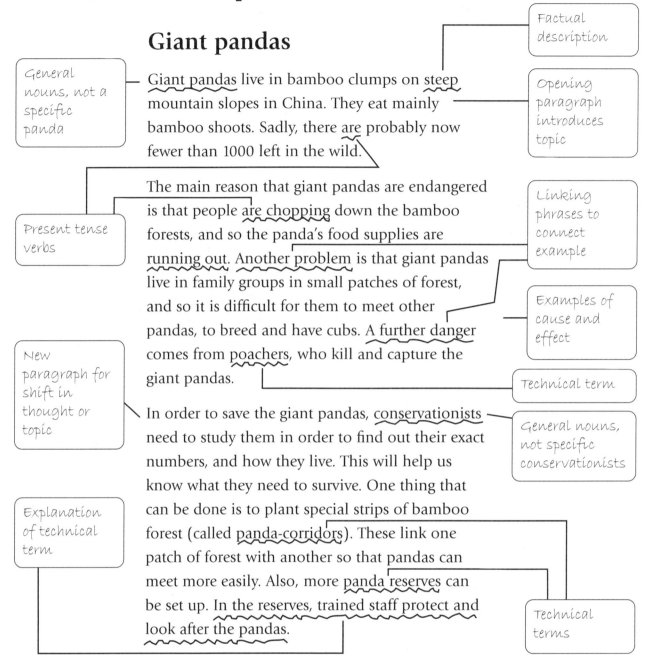

Factual description

General nouns, not a specific panda

Giant pandas live in bamboo clumps on steep mountain slopes in China. They eat mainly bamboo shoots. Sadly, there are probably now fewer than 1000 left in the wild.

Opening paragraph introduces topic

Present tense verbs

The main reason that giant pandas are endangered is that people are chopping down the bamboo forests, and so the panda's food supplies are running out. Another problem is that giant pandas live in family groups in small patches of forest, and so it is difficult for them to meet other pandas, to breed and have cubs. A further danger comes from poachers, who kill and capture the giant pandas.

Linking phrases to connect example

Examples of cause and effect

New paragraph for shift in thought or topic

In order to save the giant pandas, conservationists need to study them in order to find out their exact numbers, and how they live. This will help us know what they need to survive. One thing that can be done is to plant special strips of bamboo forest (called panda-corridors). These link one patch of forest with another so that pandas can meet more easily. Also, more panda reserves can be set up. In the reserves, trained staff protect and look after the pandas.

Technical term

General nouns, not specific conservationists

Explanation of technical term

Technical terms

Content and organization of the report text

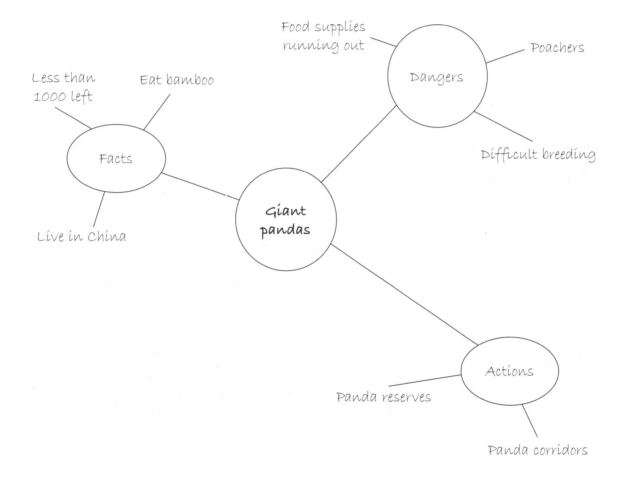

Teaching pupils how to read and write explanation text

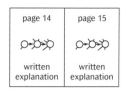

page 14	page 15
written explanation	written explanation

Reading an explanation text

Read pp 14–15 of *Improving the Environment* pupils' book with the pupils. You will need:

- the written explanation on pp 14–15 (the text-only version on p 33 of these notes can be enlarged/photocopied/made into an OHT for annotation);
- p 32 of these notes enlarged/photocopied/made into an OHT for annotation.

Audience and purpose

SHARED READING ACTIVITY

Note how the intended audience and purpose affects language and layout.

Audience – pupils who may know little about the subject.

Purpose – to provide a simple explanation of how waste is disposed of in landfill sites.

Content and organization

SHARED WRITING ACTIVITY

Revise the content and help pupils investigate how explanation text is organized by showing the text as an explanation skeleton (see p 35 of these notes). To ensure they understand the concepts, ask the pupils to produce their own explanation skeletons without looking at the book.

Language features and style

SHARED READING ACTIVITY

Return to the text and help pupils investigate the way language has been used to achieve the effects the author intended (see annotated example on p 34 of these notes). Collect any useful language features for later use in pupils' own writing, e.g. words showing the sequence of the process, (first, next, gradually) or cause and effect (although, therefore, when). Also note other features: opening statement – clear, precise language; generalized nouns, e.g. the object.

Discuss other examples of explanation text that you have shared with the class.

INDEPENDENT READING ACTIVITY

Pairs of pupils swap their skeletons with each other and read the notes. Then discuss whether they have encapsulated all the necessary points.

page 18	page 19
○→☆→⚭	○→☆→⚭
visual explanation	visual explanation

Writing an explanation text

Use pp 18–19 of *Improving the Environment* pupils' book as a basis for pupils' own explanation texts. You will need:

◆ the visual explanation on pp 18–19;
◆ p 32 of these notes enlarged/photocopied/made into an OHT for annotation.

Content and organization

Revise the content and organization of the explanation text from the previous section (see p 30 of these notes).

> **PAIRED READING AND WRITING ACTIVITY**

Ask pupils in pairs to discuss the visual flowcharts. Ask the pupils to choose either 'glass' or 'paper' and decide which point in the flow chart would be suitable as a starting point for the process of recycling.

Then ask the pairs to report back and compare their findings with the rest of the class.

Ask the pupils to make notes, thinking about how the information is going to be arranged in paragraphs.

Language features and style

Revise the main features of explanation text (see p 32 of these notes) and discuss the writing task.

Audience and purpose

Audience – readers who know little or nothing about how products can be recycled.

> **SHARED WRITING ACTIVITY**

Purpose – a written explanation of the recycling process, using either glass or paper.

Discuss the title. Should it be a statement or a question?

Model writing an opening sentence or question, e.g. *Recycling is a way of cutting down waste by re-using certain materials.*

Discuss the choice of words that could introduce the next paragraph.

Scribe the first two sentences using the pupils' suggestions.

Ask the pairs to continue the first paragraph, e.g.

Have you ever wondered how glass is recycled?
When someone has finished with a bottle or jar, instead of throwing it in the dustbin, the glass can be taken to a bottle bank. The bottle or jar should be washed first, and then put into the bottle bank according to its colour.

> **INDEPENDENT WRITING ACTIVITY**

Pupils can then write up the remaining paragraphs independently, based on the language features and structure identified by the explanation skeleton.

About explanation text

Audience and purpose

Audience – someone who wants to understand the process (how or why it happens).

Purpose – to explain how or why something happens.

> Sometimes you may know more about the age or interests of your reader

Content and organization

- **title** often asks a question, or says clearly what the explanation is about
- text often opens with **general statement(s)** to introduce important words or ideas
- the process is then written in a **series of logical steps**, usually in **time order**
- sometimes picture(s) or diagram(s)

> This happens...then this happens... next...

Language features

- **third person** writing to make the explanation **impersonal and formal**
- written in the **present tense**
- usually **general nouns and pronouns** (not particular people or things)
- **factual descriptive words**, not like the descriptions in a story
- **technical words and phrases** –which you may need to explain to the reader
- words and devices that show **sequence**
- words and devices that show **cause and effect**

> You would say old quarries not rugged ancient quarries

> You would write about waste in general, not a particular piece of rubbish

> Unusual words that go with the topic such as, canine, translucent and wingspan

> First..., next..., finally

> If..., then... This happens because... This means that...

The basic skeleton for making notes is a flowchart

> The explanation skeleton can change depending on the sort of process

An example of an explanation text

Now you see it, now you don't

Most waste in Britain goes to landfills. These are enormous holes in the ground (often old quarries). First the hole has to be lined with plastic and clay so that it is waterproof, because when waste is rotting it makes a liquid, called leachate. Leachate contains poisonous chemicals that harm the environment if they escape. Rotting waste also gives off a gas called landfill gas. This gas includes carbon dioxide and methane. These are 'greenhouse gases' which can pollute the atmosphere and lead to global warming.

When the landfill is lined, lorries tip waste into one section of it. Next, landfill compactors (machines like bulldozers, weighing 25 tonnes) spread the waste out evenly and squash it flat. When a section is full, it is covered with earth and another section is filled.

When the landfill is completely filled it is first covered with a layer of clay, which is waterproof, and then with soil, so that grass, shrubs and trees can be planted. The waste takes over 30 years to rot down, and all that time the leachate and landfill gas have to be collected and disposed of. Leachate is either treated in a sewage plant, or is made safe on site. Landfill gas is usually either burnt in flares, or burnt to provide heat or to make electricity.

Language features and style of the explanation text

Now you see it, now you don't

General features
- Consistent use of present tense
- General nouns throughout

Clear opening statement

Technical words and phrases

Words that show a sequence

Statement of cause and effect

Most waste in Britain goes to landfills. These are enormous holes in the ground (often old quarries). First the hole has to be lined with plastic and clay so that it is waterproof, because when waste is rotting it makes a liquid, called leachate. Leachate contains poisonous chemicals that harm the environment if they escape. Rotting waste also gives off a gas called landfill gas. This gas includes carbon dioxide and methane. These are 'greenhouse gases' which can pollute the atmosphere and lead to global warming.

Generalization

Causal connective

Technical term

When the landfill is lined, lorries tip waste into one section of it. Next, landfill compactors (machines like bulldozers, weighing 25 tonnes) spread the waste out evenly and squash it flat. When a section is full, it is covered with earth and another section is filled.

Definitions of terms included to help understanding

When the landfill is completely filled it is first covered with clay, which is waterproof, and then with soil, so that grass, shrubs and trees can be planted. The waste takes over 30 years to rot down, and all that time the leachate and landfill gas have to be collected and disposed of. Leachate is either treated in a sewage plant, or is made safe on site. Landfill gas is usually either burnt in flares, or burnt to provide heat or to make electricity.

Technical vocabulary

Generalization

If you are using this text with other year groups then also highlight these features:

Y3/P4
◆ Collective nouns and singular/plural verbs (**waste is**).
◆ Compound words (**landfill, waterproof**).

Y5/P6
◆ The use of punctuation in complex sentences.
◆ The inclusion of technical definitions within the text.

Y6/P7
◆ More sophisticated punctuation (brackets).
◆ Impersonal style.
◆ Complex sentences using causal conjunctions.

Content and organization of the explanation text

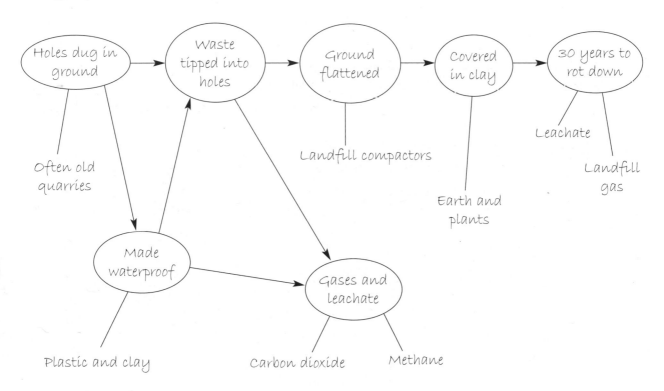

Teaching pupils how to read and write persuasion text

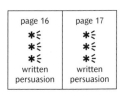

page 16	page 17
✳ ≥	✳ ≥
✳ ≥	✳ ≥
✳ ≥	✳ ≥
written persuasion	written persuasion

Reading a persuasion text

Read pp 16–17 of *Improving the Environment* pupils' book with the pupils. You will need:

- the persuasion text on pp 16–17 (the text-only version on p 39 of these notes can be enlarged/photocopied/made into an OHT for annotation);
- p 38 of these notes enlarged/photocopied/made into an OHT for annotation.

> SHARED READING ACTIVITY

Audience and purpose

Talk about how the intended audience and purpose affects language and layout.

Audience – the recipient of the letter; people with the ability to take action on an issue.

Purpose – to persuade someone to take action about an issue.

> SHARED READING ACTIVITY

Content and organization

Show the pupils how the content of the letters are organized by showing the content in a persuasion skeleton (see p 41 of these notes). Each main point is listed with elaboration or explanation linked to it.

> SHARED READING ACTIVITY

> SHARED WRITING ACTIVITY

Language features and style

Return to the text and talk about the way the language has been used to achieve the effect the author intended (see annotated version on p 40).

Note useful features for pupils' own writing, e.g. formal or informal tone of language and style chosen to suit the intended audience, emotional language, concluding sentence is a call to action, *So tell . . ., Please, can you . . .*

Add other examples provided by the pupils.

> INDEPENDENT ACTIVITY

In pairs, choose a letter and the reply and act it out as a conversation. Discuss the difference in style and methods of emphasizing the persuasive points.

Writing persuasion text

Use pp 40–41 of *Improving the Environment* pupils' book as a basis for pupils' own persuasive advertisements. You will need:

◆ the advertisements on pp 40–41 of the pupils' book;
◆ p 38 of these notes enlarged/photocopied/made into an OHT for annotation.

Content and organization

Revise the content and organization of persuasion text from the previous session (see p 36 of these notes).

> PAIRED READING ACTIVITY

Pairs of pupils read and compare the advertisements, looking for devices to attract the readers' attention, emotive vocabulary, the different 'calls to take action' and how they vary according to the intended effect of the advertisement.

Language features of persuasion texts

> SHARED READING ACTIVITY

Remind the pupils of the language features of persuasion text (see p 38 of these notes).

Audience and purpose

> SHARED READING ACTIVITY

Discuss the audience and purpose for pupils' persuasion texts (people who you wish to influence) and purpose (to influence the reader to act in a certain way).

Remind the pupils how the intended audience affects the choice of language, tone and vocabulary.

> SHARED WRITING ACTIVITY

With the pupils, decide on an issue that is relevant to their interests and experience, e.g. traffic outside school, local river pollution, dog dirt on pavements, etc.

Demonstrate how to write an eye-catching sentence or phrase. Discuss how much information is needed. Scribe some of the pupils' suggestions and discuss which ones are the most effective and why.

> PAIRED WRITING ACTIVITY

Pairs of pupils make notes of what information to include by compiling a persuasion skeleton.

Discuss the layout of the advertisements, and experiment with different styles, e.g. narrative, bullet points, text boxes, etc.

> SHARED WRITING ACTIVITY

Discuss the language style, and whether commands (imperative verbs), requests or rhetorical questions will have the desired impact.

> INDEPENDENT WRITING ACTIVITY

Pupils write their own persuasion advertisements.

About persuasion text

Audience and purpose

Audience – someone you want to persuade, but who may not know much about the subject.

Purpose – to argue the case for a point of view, persuade someone to buy something or support a cause.

> Sometimes you may know more about the age or interests of your reader

Content and organization

- usually starts with a sentence or paragraph to **introduce the argument**
- the argument is then split into a number of **main points,** each of which probably needs some **elaboration**
- **concluding sentence or paragraph** sums up the argument

> You may have to introduce some important words or ideas the reader needs to know

> The elaboration could be
> – reasons for agreeing with the point
> – examples to back it up
> – further information to explain it

Language features

- writing may be personal (**first and second person**) or impersonal (**third person**)
- written in the **present tense**
- language may be quite **emotional,** more like a story than other non-fiction
- there may be **rhetorical questions,** which do not really expect an answer
- words and devices showing **cause and effect,** used to **argue** the case
- words and devices that show movement from one point to the next

> Use powerful verbs and adjectives, exaggerations or repetition to make an effect

> Is this really important?

> Therefore . . ., Consequently . . ., This means that . . .

> Firstly . . ., Another reason that . . ., Thirdly . . .

The basic skeleton for making notes is pronged bullet points

An example of persuasion text

Dear Sir or Madam

Our road is very noisy. There is a lot of traffic on it, especially in the morning when people are going to work or school, and in the evening when they are coming home.

During the day big lorries use the road a lot. They are sometimes so noisy that they make our house shake, and all the windows rattle. My little brother finds it scary, because our old house didn't do that.

Another thing – the traffic sometimes wakes us up in the middle of the night. There is a pothole outside our house, and when the lorries fall in it, they make a loud CLUNK. The empty gravel lorries are especially bad. Sometimes I can't get back to sleep, and then I feel very tired at school.

Please, can you make our road quieter?

Yours faithfully

Chloe Goodchild

Language features and style of a persuasion text

Directly addressing the reader

Dear Sir or Madam

Clear opening statement of the main point

Our road is very noisy. There is a lot of traffic on it, especially in the morning when people are going to work or school, and in the evening when they are coming home.

Elaboration of main point

During the day big lorries use the road a lot. They are sometimes so noisy that they make our house shake, and all the windows rattle. My little brother finds it scary, because our old house didn't do that.

Statement of cause and effect

Emotional language

Present tense verb

Moving to a further point

Another thing – the traffic sometimes wakes us up in the middle of the night. There is a pothole outside our house, and when the lorries fall in it, they make a loud CLUNK. The empty gravel lorries are especially bad. Sometimes I can't get back to sleep, and then I feel very tired at school.

Font use for effect

Emotional language

Closing request to take action

Please, can you make our road quieter?

Yours faithfully

Chloe Goodchild

If you are using this text with other year groups then also highlight these features:

Y3/P4   ◆ Style, layout and vocabulary in letters.

Y5/P6   ◆ Degree of formality, vocabulary and tone.
           ◆ Opinion versus fact.

Y6/P7   ◆ Connectives used to link thoughts, paragraphs.

Content and organization of the persuasion text

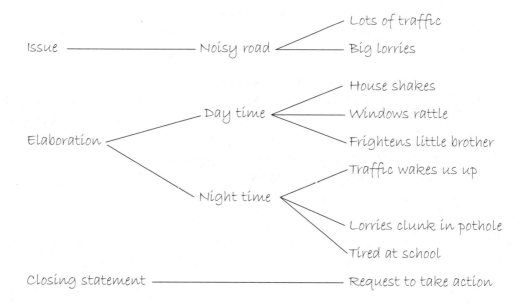

Teaching pupils how to read and write discussion text

page 43

written discussion

Reading a discussion text

Read p 43 of *Improving the Environment* pupils' book with the pupils. You will need:

- the written discussion text on p 43 (the text-only version on p 45 of these notes can be enlarged/photocopied/made into an OHT for annotation);
- p 44 of these notes enlarged/photocopied/made into an OHT for annotation.

SHARED
READING
ACTIVITY

Audience and purpose
Note how the intended audience and purpose affects language and layout.

Audience – school pupils who may not have thought about the issue previously.

Purpose – to stimulate discussion on the issue.

SHARED
WRITING
ACTIVITY

Content and organization
Revise the content and help pupils recognize how discussion text is organized by showing the content as a discussion skeleton (see p 47 of these notes).

SHARED
READING
ACTIVITY

Language features and style
Return to the text and help pupils investigate how the language has been used to achieve the effects the author intended (annotated example on p 46 of these notes). Collect any useful language features for pupils' later use, and add others from pupils' own experience, e.g. words denoting two sides to an argument, *On the other hand, this means that, alternatively, etc.*

INDEPENDENT
ACTIVITY

In groups, brainstorm better forms of transport for getting around cities.

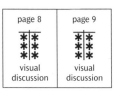
Writing a discussion text

Use pp 8–9 of *Improving the Environment* pupils' book as a basis for pupils' own discussion texts. You will need:

◆ the visual discussion on pp 8–9;
◆ p 44 of these notes enlarged/photocopied/made into an OHT for annotation.

Content and organization

Revise the content and organization of discussion text from the previous session (see p 42 of these notes).

> **PAIRED READING ACTIVITY**

Ask pupils in pairs to read the discussion and identify the two different viewpoints, i.e. litter, anti-litter. Ask some pairs to explain the points for litter, and others the anti-litter points.

Ask the pupils to transfer the points in the discussion onto a discussion skeleton.

Language features of discussion texts

Revise the main language features of discussion texts on p 45 of these notes.

> **SHARED READING ACTIVITY**

Re-visit the list of language features from the previous session and add any others from the pupils' suggestions that relate to the writing task.

Discuss the verb tenses used, and model how to change one of the first person sentences into the third person to make the discussion impersonal.

Audience and purpose

Discuss the audience for the pupils' leaflet (other school pupils) and the purpose (to raise awareness of litter in the playground).

> **SHARED WRITING ACTIVITY**

Demonstrate writing an introductory sentence to state the issue, e.g. *At the end of playtime the playground is strewn with litter.*

Discuss the order of the points to be included in the leaflet, e.g. should they be written as alternating for and against points, or all the for points together followed by the opposing points?

Scribe some of the pupils' suggestions, and allow the pupils to make their own decisions on how to structure their leaflets.

> **INDEPENDENT WRITING ACTIVITY**

Pupils write up their own leaflets, using the notes on their discussion skeletons as a basis.

About discussion text

Audience and purpose

Audience – someone who wants to know both sides of the argument, but may not know much about the subject.

Purpose – to present arguments and information from different viewpoints.

Sometimes you may know more about the age or interests of your reader

Content and organization

- usually starts with a sentence or paragraph **introducing the subject** under discussion and **defining important terms**
- the argument is then split into a number of **main points for and against**
- the arguments for and against are supported by **evidence and examples**
- **concluding sentence or paragraph** sums up the main points, for and against (and sometimes expresses the author's own opinions)

Introduce important words or ideas the reader needs to know

You can either give all the arguments for, then all the arguments against, or all arguments for and against each point – one by one

The examples could:
- agree with the point
- back up the evidence
- add further information to explain it

Language features

- written in the **third person** to make the discussion **impersonal and formal**
- usually in the **present tense**
- usually **generalized nouns** (except in specific examples)
- words and devices showing **cause and effect,** used to **argue** the case
- words and devices that signal a **move from one side of the argument** to the other
- words and devices which suggest 'possibility' rather than certainty

Give the people on each side names, such as Supporters claim..., Critics reply...

Environmentalists, developers, scientists...

Therefore..., Consequently..., This means that...

However..., On the other hand...

Perhaps..., probably..., might..., could be...

The basic skeleton for making notes is a for-and-against grid

An example of a discussion text

The environment is for everyone ... but that doesn't mean everyone can do what they want

The boy on the skateboard wants to jump down the steps. The little children want to climb up the steps. What will happen?

If the boy goes on he will knock the children over. Then not only will the children be hurt, but they will lie in his way, crying, and he won't be able to skateboard at all. So he waits until the children are out of his way, and then does his jump – or else he skateboards somewhere else.

Change

Cars are designed to travel from one place to another quickly and easily. However, there are very often traffic jams going into towns and cities. In a traffic jam nobody goes anywhere, or they just move very slowly. Pollution comes out of exhaust pipes: gases and dust that can make people ill, and carbon dioxide which contributes to global warming. Are drivers aware of what they are doing? It is as if the boy had decided to knock the little children over, but instead of the children, it is the environment that is hurt and crying.

We all share the environment, and sometimes we need to give up, or change, things that we want to do, in order for the environment to survive. We need to come up with new, bright and exciting ways of doing things better. Can you think of a better form of transport to take the place of cars in towns and cities?

Language features and style of the discussion text

Title introduces the topic for discussion

The environment is for everyone . . . but that doesn't mean everyone can do what they want

The boy on the skateboard wants to jump down the steps. The little children want to climb up the steps. What will happen?

Language of cause and effect

If the boy goes on he will knock the children over. Then not only will the children be hurt, but they will lie in his way, crying, and he won't be able to skateboard at all. So he waits until the children are out of his way, and then does his jump – or else he skateboards somewhere else.

Impersonal third person

Change

Cars are designed to travel from one place to another quickly and easily. However there are very often traffic jams going into towns and cities. In a traffic jam nobody goes anywhere, or they just move very slowly. Pollution comes out of exhaust pipes: gases and dust that can make people ill, and carbon dioxide which contributes to global warming. Are drivers aware of what they are doing? It is as if the boy had decided to knock the little children over, but instead of the children, it is the environment that is hurt and crying.

Generalized nouns

Connective signals move to other side of argument

Definition of terms

Use of questions invites readers to think of answers

We all share the environment, and sometimes we need to give up, or change, things that we want to do, in order for the environment to survive. We need to come up with new, bright and exciting ways of doing things better. Can you think of a better form of transport to take the place of cars in towns and cities?

Connective used to argue the case

Move to first person plural makes closing statement inclusive

Final direct question moves language from impersonal to personal

If you are using this text with other year groups then also highlight these features:

Y3/P4 ◆ The differences between verbs in 1st, 2nd and 3rd person.

Y5/P6 ◆ Adapting writing for different purposes, using auxiliary verbs.

Y6/P7 ◆ Connectives

Content and organization of the discussion text

It is ok to do what you want	It is not ok to do what you want
◆ It's fun to skateboard down steps	◆ Other people need to use the steps
◆ Skateboarders need somewhere to practise – jumps and steps cost nothing	◆ You will be in serious trouble if you knock a child over
◆ Cars get you quickly to places	◆ Traffic jams stop you getting to places on time
◆ Traffic jams mean cars move slowly which means fewer people are in danger	◆ You waste fuel while waiting in traffic jams, and fossil fuels are a non-renewable source of energy
	◆ While you are in a traffic jam, your exhaust sends gases into the air
	◆ Exhaust fumes damage the environment

Page	Contents	Text type	National Literacy Strategy Objectives	QCA Geography Objectives Unit 8
				Pupils should learn:
2	Concept map and Contents	Reference		
4	What is the environment?	Visual report	T1 TL 16, 17, 18, 27 T1 WL 2,3	• to ask and respond to geographical questions
6	Why do we need to improve our environment?	Visual explanation	T2 18, 19, 20, 21, 22, 24, 25 T2 WL 2, 3, 11	• how people affect the environment • how and why people seek to manage and sustain their environment
8	What a mess!	Visual persuasion	T3 16, 17, 18, 19, 20, 21, 22, 24 T3 SL 2, 4	
10	Clean it up!	Visual persuasion	T3 16, 17, 18, 19, 20, 21, 22, 23, 24, 25 T3 SL 2, 4 T3 WL 2, 3	
12	Dealing with problems – looking at traffic	Written recount Written instruction		• to ask and respond to geographical questions • to collect and record evidence to answer questions
14	Now you see it, now you don't	Written explanation	T2 18, 19, 20, 21, 22, T2 WL 11	• how people affect the environment • how and why people seek to manage and sustain their environment
16	This must stop!	Written persuasion	T3 16, 17, 18, 19, 20, 21, 22, 23, 24, 25 T3 SL 2, 4 T3 WL 2, 3	• how and why people seek to manage and sustain their environment • to collect and record evidence to answer questions
18	Recycling	Visual explanation	T2 18, 19, 20, 21, 22, 24, 25 T2 WL 2, 3, 11	
20	How to make compost/ Look carefully!	Written instruction Written report	T1 TL 16, 17, 18, T1 WL 2,3	
22	Air pollution	Written recount Visual persuasion	T2 18, 19, 20, 21, 22, T2 WL 11	• to collect and record evidence to answer questions • how and why people seek to manage and sustain their environment
24	Up in the air	Written discussion Written explanation	T2 18, 19, 20, 21, 22, 24, 25 T2 WL 2, 3, 11	• to ask and respond to geographical questions • how people affect the environment • to collect and record evidence to answer questions • how and why people seek to manage and sustain their environment
26	People are not the only problem	Visual report Written report Journalistic recount	T1 TL 20, 21, 24 T1 WL 2,3	• to collect and record evidence to answer questions • to investigate places
28	Rivers and beaches	Visual recount	T1 TL 16, 17, 18, 27 T1 WL 2,3	• to ask and respond to geographical questions • to collect and record evidence to answer questions • how people affect the environment • how and why people seek to manage and sustain their environment
30	Land use	Written report Visual explanation	T2 18, 19, 20, 21, 22, 24, 25 T2 WL 2, 3, 11	• to ask and respond to geographical questions • how people affect the environment • to collect and record evidence to answer questions • to use ICT to present findings
32	Animals in danger	Written and Visual report	T1 TL 16, 17, 18, 27 T1 WL 2,3	• how people affect the environment • how and why people seek to manage and sustain their environment
34	International and national action	Written report Written persuasion	T1 TL 20, 21, 24 T1 WL 2,3 T3 16, 17, 18, 19, 20, 21, 22, 23, 24, 25 T3 SL 2, 4 T3 WL 2, 3	• how and why people seek to manage and sustain their environment • to investigate places
36	Community action	Written and Visual report	T1 TL 20, 21, 24 T1 WL 2,3	• how and why people seek to manage and sustain their environment
38	Building a wildlife garden	Visual instruction	T1 TL 16, 17, 18, 22 T1 SL 2	• how and why people seek to manage and sustain their environment • to collect and record evidence to answer questions
40	Stop press	Visual persuasion	T3 16, 17, 18, 19, 20, 21, 22, 24 T3 SL 2, 4	• to collect and record evidence to answer questions • how and why people seek to manage and sustain their environment • to investigate places • to ask and respond to geographical questions • how people affect the environment
42	The environment is for everyone …	Visual report Written discussion	T1 TL 16, 17, 18, 27 T1 WL 2,3	
44	What now?	Visual report Written persuasion	T3 16, 17, 18, 19, 20, 21, 22, 23, 24, 25 T3 SL 2, 4 T3 WL 2, 3	• how people affect the environment • how and why people seek to manage and sustain their environment • to investigate places
46	Glossary	Reference		• to ask are respond to geographical questions
47	Bibliography	Reference		• to collect and record evidence to answer questions
48	Index	Reference		